EVER AFTER

EVER AFTER

POEMS

FRED CHAPPELL

Louisiana State University Press
Baton Rouge

Published by Louisiana State University Press
lsupress.org

Designer: Emma R. Theodore
Typefaces: Adobe Caslon Pro, text; Baskerville, display.

Cover photograph courtesy Unsplash.com / Kirk Thornton.

Library of Congress Cataloging-in-Publication Data

Names: Chappell, Fred, 1936–2024, author.
Title: Ever after : poems / Fred Chappell.
Description: Baton Rouge : Louisiana State University Press, 2024.
Identifiers: LCCN 2024013747 (print) | LCCN 2024013748 (ebook) |
    ISBN 978-0-8071-8260-4 (paperback) | ISBN 978-0-8071-8354-0 (epub) |
    ISBN 978-0-8071-8355-7 (pdf)
Subjects: LCGFT: Poetry.
Classification: LCC PS3553.H298 E94 2024 (print) | LCC PS3553.H298 (ebook) |
    DDC 811/.54—dc23/eng/20240329
LC record available at https://lccn.loc.gov/2024013747
LC ebook record available at https://lccn.loc.gov/2024013748

for Michiko Stavert

CONTENTS

EVER AFTER

A SMALLER NIGHT MUSIC

The trees give all to their casual artistries:
The brawny black oak stalwart in Lindley Park
gathers sunlight into its patterned shadow,
amassing in heaps the spendthrift solar downpour
until the largo sundown brings slow peace
and these absented acres welcome the dark.
Tomorrow will freshen the grove and patient meadow,
the dawn will bring once more its deceptive candor.
And now the night arrives and flows into
the shadow of the tree and draws it forth.
The daytime music it absorbed sounds out:
butterflies trilling gaily as they weave about,
the pebbled stream warbling its way through earth,
the silent tremolo shimmer of the dew.

AUBADE

Waking, we are parted, denuded driftwood
cast upon the silver beach of morning
by the exhausted energies of darkness.
We now are two who in the night were one.

Daylight disfigures us with identity;
we see each other now as other.
You are attired in your individual form,
discarding the unshaped figure of timeless hours.

Now you are one again and sport your name
like an accessory taken from a drawer
and attached to the apparent body like a scarf,
a daily badge you wear as custom requires.

The long day drains away and night reclaims
the world and "Susan" is anonymous once more,
and we are one again, unnameable,
where there is no I for eye to find.

THE DAILY GRIND

for John and Esther Lang

The duties of innocence fall to Adam and Eve.
Their Paradise is a playground of seesaws,
Swings and slides, gymsets, and whirlyhaws.
They are called upon to laugh and never grieve.

Hear them salute the peacock dawn with song;
Their meals include no flesh or fish or fowl;
They feast upon bright grapes the whole day long,
Nighttimes attend the monomelodic owl.

They are beset by purple damselflies
Transporting scraps of glitter across the hours
Of fragrant breeze and cotton-tufted skies,
Zigzag through the lanes of lank sunflowers.

They romp through endless games of hide-and-seek,
And Adam vows to Eve he will not peek.

ANONYMOUS

If Susan speaks or sings, her voice detaches
to make itself another of the various night sounds:
wind disarranging the clematis garlandry,
car horns by the stadium twelve blocks west,
barred owl violating the moon-hush.

They who leave our world despoil it with their absence;
we who speak in the night speak to the night.
Everyone who longs to say the truth
must employ the ancient words of sages.
This one night is all that ever is.
My voice transfigures into a reverent silence.

SUM TOTAL

Lost is the adjective we bestow
on things that have become anonymous
in time and over time. We claim to know
what random circumstance has brought upon us,
though now that bright event has lost its name
and every distinct feature to stand alone
amid the crowd of others all the same,
each now featureless one by one by one,
like soldiers in ranks or bottles in a shelf,
all of them together without a self,
every lonely one never alone.
They come and go and none is ever gone;
they go and come and none is ever here;
they crowd a past wherein they never were.

GUARDIANS

The senior fellow I saw on his knees
weeding his row of jonquils and white cilla
seemed as intent as Archimedes
sketching designs for an elegant umbrella.

He bent into the earth, then straightened up
to inspect some piddling green sprout he had found
between a violet and a buttercup,
marring his pristine and holy ground.

So Susan discovers an alien element
in the friendly confines of the living room:
a mote of dust, speck of invisible lint
that may presage unsanitary doom.

So here she stands, our valiant sentinel,
to send the Space Invaders straight to hell.

INTERVALS

When Psyche blows soap bubbles with her pipe
they roll and waft and double-dip the air
in graceful frolic, silent, debonair,
as if the breeze directed them to slip
in waltz time through this world that they display
as rainbows on their bright rotundities,
to celebrate each separate demise,
each sphere spritzing as it goes away.

Chronos' pipe is carved of human bone;
the bubbles he produces are misshapen,
withered like grapes by a relentless sun,
their colors dark; and it may often happen
they disappear as soon as they appear
and mark no time to tell they ever were.

REMINDERS

The pieces of itself the sky
hurls at us continually—
the mythological starlight,
the homeless orphan meteorite,
silken visions of hazy galaxies,
jetsam of immaterial seas—
these we receive as cool reminder
that every light will shrink to cinder.

ORPHEUS

The nameless brook twinkled through the narrow valley,
sounding a various music, sleepily modulating,
endlessly warbling, beneath the wafted gowns of willows.

I lay with my eyes closed beside the mossy water.
Music filled my universe and all the others
and then fell silent but for an echo and its undertone.

My age was a thousand years of adolescence,
I was old as the brook but never as wise,
as wise as music but never so young.
I vowed to master the harp when it came to be discovered,
to embrace my fate and my fateful love,

      to make of the world a lamentation.

TEACHER

The evergreen expands its mass
but not its angel figuration;
its stateliness remains unchanged.
In December we stroll the grove
where a peaceful balsam spreads the sod
with a comforter of quiet needles.

The Seer does not comprehend
the mission that has overtaken his every hour.
He wears a threadbare cloak in which he wanders
the watchful world as a friendly stranger,
consoling without permission its prisoners.

LIMBO GALLERY

Whenever you enter Limbo the marble figures
examine you with watchful eyes unmoved,
impersonating those you desired to be,
the daring Philosopher, Physician beloved,
the Soldier enwreathed by beaming Victory,
the studious Saint whom loneliness transfigures.

Some stand here you do not recognize:
the polished Diplomat, the Orgiast
disdained by women as an unsocial beast,
the frothing Zealot with his wig ablaze.
Yet these and others in the revealing guise
of stale ambitions represent at last
forlorn ideals of life you coveted most
and hold you fixed in their indifferent gaze.

ALTERNATE VISION

When the unicorn was revealed unto the saint
the animal stood as in a pose: the head
upraised, the horn tilting slightly sunward,
the left front hoof disdaining the grassy turf,
and the tail a swish of silver silk breeze-swept.

The holy man memorized every detail,
foreknowing this vision never would return.
From now forever he must content himself
with images of angels and of the Virgin,
of heaven's portal and the gates of hell,
and other stock backdrops for revelation,
reverent but maybe a little shopworn.

ICON

Her name does not return who said to me,
"Poems are how we see with our eyes closed."
She was a handsome girl. She closed her eyes,
as if to demonstrate her manifesto,
but then fell silent, expecting me to know
her sentence and her silence calmly composed
the poem she carried with her everywhere
as she traversed her valiant nineteenth year.

For watchful moments she stood in the buzzing hallway
in loosely belted skirt and cross-thong sandals,
as if she occupied a separate place,
windy, sunblown, filled with skimming swallows,
a space wherein an artist might draw a prophet
who wordlessly foretells our every sorrow.

UPON REFLECTION

The lake draws the trees and sky upon itself.
Thus it overfills with images and rises
toward the shores as if fed by secret springs.
It is a world clothing itself with another world,
as a woman pulls on a kimono painted with springtime.

A quarter moon passes over, leaving its imprint
in the form of waves that lap the shore,
in the crescent shape of wind-ripple shadows.
All the surface seizes, it silences.
The lake depicts our world cleansed of its uproar
to demonstrate a holier state of being,
peaceful and contemplative, immune to time,
one further paradise closed to humankind.

SONG

When in my mind I look into my coffin
as one of eight attendees in a bored band of mourners,
I find the box is empty. I am elsewhere
or nowhere, occupying a private dimension
with walls not blank but calmly uninformative.
These walls enclose but do not imprison;
these walls admit the song of the mourning dove,
three soulful notes that confirm the life and the death.

STAIRWAY TO HEAVEN

We kneel upon the earth and genuflect;
we raise our voices to the blasé skies,
begging forgiveness for our disrespect,
miming the mindless public exercise.

Observe our shadows as we perform the rite:
how bodiless they all embody the grace
we share divested of our human weight,
dark spirit-beings the moon cannot efface.

Our voices soar, our prayers remain earthbound,
tethered by the stubborn ligaments
of physical function, taste and touch and sound.
We are scum-lumps of humble elements.

Do not despair. Reach toward the light divine.
In yonder cupboard stands a jug of wine.

THE LONG VIEW

And now you have enveloped the child you were
in the body that was to be, and laid aside
the questions that confused the maiden soul
to search more dangerous perplexities.
These rise as furious specters and abide
nightlong under a moon solemnly full
that drifts above and yet within the air
and pauses to engage the pensive seas.

Where is the child?—abducted by the moon.
And who are you?—I am she who ponders
past and future, catalogues the wonders
and shrouded fears, notates them one by one,
gathers each into its lonely file,
and slowly, carefully, encrypts the whole.

EFFIGY

You are imprisoned so that mind and sky
compose your universe. You wait and watch,
though you are stone that captures what can be
in a cruel immortality
silent except for your regretful sigh.

A nonexistent future inters the past
that shrouds you now in its marble winding sheet.
Whatever hope there was is found too late;
each tomorrow troubles into dust.

Memory is worst. All former joy
returns as mockery: your twelfth birthday,
your faltering first kiss, your happiest toy,
the final phrase you heard your mother say.
These remembered flames now burn afresh
to embrace your spirit, subliming it to ash.

LATER ON

The couple who have loved a long time together
share a sorrow they never name aloud.
Each imagines last years without the other,
foreseeing futures enveloped by the past,
the days and seasons lengthening each hour
into a moment time has not effaced
that forced all memory into its power.

Who is she now? she wonders. Who is he
that cannot sleep at night or wake at dawn?
They rise from bed and put their bodies on
and go about their rituals one by one,
hoping that today she might be free,
fearing that today he will be free.

THE PRACTICE OF INDIFFERENCE

Eagerly urgent, the words you whispered.

But I train myself to ignore importance,
to huff out the candle that shines upon it.

To unremember is arduous, requiring a strength
of indifference I must labor to maintain.
My indifference adorns itself with nonchalance;
often I seem to forget as easily as a cat curls on a sofa,
but this appearance of grace is hard to maintain.

Whatever you confided I will forget,
disburden myself of message as gracefully
as her partner prince lowers the ballerina
and exits stage right forever, his absence a declaration.

EYE TO EYE

There is no place upon or near you
my gaze does not still linger.
Our chronicle begins anew
when our eyes meet even by accident.

E PLURIBUS UNUM

An assembly of immortals collaborated
in your assemblage. They chose each material
according to motley design, ethereal
or dearly human, seemingly mismated
at random jointures. Thoughtful and mercurial,
your every impulse is a fleet memorial;
your attributes enmesh as if calculated
to illustrate the ways you are created.

Though you appear to be all of one piece,
Susan is no monogenic stone;
your nature flickers tipsy with caprice
and purpose; you disrupt the monotone
that shadows our fluteful music celestial:
Not all one piece, you are a piece of All.

PROSPECT

He pauses from desk-bound labor to look through
the window past the powerline
harboring four contentious crows and beyond
to where the roofs of the dingy mill village huddle
in a muted flock. He begins to speculate
upon the inner workings of the outer world:
When must the universe devour itself?

The aggressive page with his few spider-scribbles
expands to the size of a glacier,
an immense white rose petal,
eager to receive some purpose for existence.

STOP TIME

As when a hand upon the shoulder causes you to turn
and peer into the face of a forlorn stranger,
or when your bedroom closet opens to disclose
a man in a homburg with his back toward you,
so her awareness of new love startles the woman.

She feels she should withdraw from the hubbub room.
She feels that if she acknowledges the man approaching,
all that may occur can never be undone,
the future contracting to an unlit corridor.

She knows that she will not refuse the first encounter.
Her breath quickens, her gaze wanders unfixed,
as if tracing a butterfly that skips and pauses
among the garden blooms a breeze impersonally fondles.

But is he coming to her, moving gracefully across the room
through the brandished cocktails and muddled faces?
Maybe he comes to greet the mayor's son, who stands
behind her.

Maybe not.

REMODELING

The remodeling of a neighbor's decrepit house:
thumping of lumber, chirring of sanders,
radio love songs in lilting español.
We are reminded of the valiant ladies
swimming at the Y, imploring the return of youth,
as hopeful as the eight-year-old addressing her piano.

In our old house the silence is not expectant.
The wallpaper fades with a sound like dreamless sleep.
The veteran cat protects her favored corner.
The washer completes its task and signals.
One of us turns one thousand years old.

STORAGE

The several childhoods Loma stored away
in an attic trunk lie listening to the rain
or silent snow all through the night and day
and year and season. Time may come again
for some of them to reinvest the memory
of this and that, and him, and where and when,
all now enjambed in one discordancy,
diminuendo chord to single tone.

Yes, she recalls the ragged Raggedy Ann,
Scarlett O'Hara in her original box,
Barbie in shorts minus insipid Ken,
the blue-eyed, chipped, and legless Goldilocks,
the tiny, twisted one she will not name
who visits and revisits a lonesome dream.

THE DREAMS

In the night they fly silently across the nation,
inspecting the minds of sleepers one by one
like swallows searching out nesting spots
or graceful dark ospreys scouting prey.

Now and again they invade spaces uncultivated,
transforming the turbulent mute environments
into abundant worlds colorful with terror
and musical as wind chimes strung along the seashore.

So thoroughly do they occupy the sleepers' amazement
that when sunlight draws the dreams away
their traces remain, indecipherable, indelible,
stippling their vistas with omens and ruins.

And now the sleepers rise to attend their various errands,
plundering forward into dream after daylit dream.

RELIC

Forlorn it stands amid the attic clutter,
a lonesome sonnet in cobweb disrepair;
about its base the deft mice squeak and scutter;
its shadow melds with other shadows here.
Octave has lost its wonted stateliness;
anapests have squirmed into some lines
where sturdy iambs formerly held sway;
abrupt spondees confuse the calm designs
of breve, accent, and silent caesurae.

The sestet is a threadbare afterthought.
Three whole lines remain and broken phrases
that may or may not fittingly conjoin
      where nightjars
               abide the starshine
and Hy[pn]os.

WITNESS

I study intently, but no history reveals its import.
The past guards its instances like a mother
who shields her children from the drunken husband.

The ancient betrayals maintain their integrities,
holding like confessionals their shames in silence.

The abyss between then and now guarantees all witness
untrustworthy, yet still your eyes accuse me.

           Yet still your eyes

TIME

The name of an unsought future comes to this young girl,
Soundless and formless,
With power gathered from her uncertainty.

At first she compares it to a flower unfolding,
An image her innocence approves,
Yet maybe it is like a sweet and silver wine
A spiny season of the moon may tum to poison,
And they will change together, she and her first love,
And the moon will shorten the seasons of her every love:

As the colors of one love tint all other colors,
So the first new tentative kisses cannot cancel
All her former ecstasies and their attendant sorrows.

TIME AFTER TIME

As toward the shoreline of a summer lake
A rower toiling solitary onward looks back to find
Her former life receded, indistinct,
A smear of colors and an echo over water:
So the woman seeks to recall her first love and her second.

When love was young she feared its strength
Might derive from a sweet and silver poison.
How could her heart be true if she never understood
The force that worked upon her and within?

Her passion was always to be the person she demanded to be.
She follows where long love has taken her,
Out upon this lonesome water where the day-moon
Lays down its reflection like a poker chip
In desperate wager against the past and the viewless future.

AND TIME AGAIN

We shall lie down, woman and man and child
And every elder, to make peace,
More simply than we had thought, with the final ocean
That draws the ragged cloak of tide upon us.

"Is that a signal light," someone will say,
"Swaying its brightness and its shadow in the far tower?"
A woman shall hear a voice long forgotten.
A child shall cry out to be less forlorn.
An aged man shall imagine his strength regained
As he descends to the deepest current.

These events shall happen in a later age,
Yet now already it is time to attend,
As within the stubborn clatter of the world
A silence begins to out-curl like an ink drop in water,
As within the blood of a young girl
A shy warmth begins to tell she is in love.

TIME OUT OF MIND

And so the night has come for her to be an aged woman.
With shadow shaping shadow, the November moon
Slimming and enlarging in the dormer window,
She counts some names of loves the years have not unspelled.

Her past and future have been conditional:
Both are possibilities for loss and love,
Both present in the mind that watches midnight
Display its shopworn moon, then take it down again.
Remembrance saves what time destroys, for a time.

There comes, as it may come to all, the certainty
That a human season is merely human, a matter
Of being so confused with love that even death
Cannot define what thing it is. Time does not engulf
This hour or comfort it with promise of oblivion.

TIMEWROUGHT

She feels the November midnight knows her truly,
searching forcibly the bitter sources
of one despairing love and then another,
the moonless sky a mirror of the moment
that darkened every moment from then till ever.
The lonesomer the night the more she feels it
shrouding about her like a worn-out topcoat,
as patched with mends as an hour with memories.

And then there was a woman Margaret
whom she now recognized as Margaret,
created from and by the ruin of time,
as the first Margaret to cast a shadow
by her own light and stand within that light.
Her past exists now only as the past,
sealed away from her as in a vault.
The more she has, no was, the more she is.

TIME WHEN

The woman pauses her needle and stares before her.
Silently she comes to know a man she loved
In sudden years gone by has died. From him she learned
The many thousand ways the world is not.

Strange, how the power of memory increases
When objects of its longing are taken away.
Strange, that the woman has no power to weep.

For half an hour she sits alone, examining
The shapeless silence with its dark message,
And then she puts her sewing by and rises to address
New ceremonies of her altered life,
To bear her sorrow gracefully, as a tree bears snow.

PAUSE

Time now to ship the oars and drift.
Sunset tints the lake orange and silver.
Heron retreats into the stand of sparse bamboo,
adding her absence to the nearly silent hour.
Your pensive smile suggests that you recall
some moment past, a cello sonata passage,
your mother fingering through her recipe file,
a gentle hand placed on your shoulder when Tabby died.

MOMENT

Is now the sad betrayal she feels it is?
Gavin has signed to join the Marines.
His dad gained medals for disabilities;
his uncle Max fought in the Philippines
but that was then. Can he not comprehend
how she will darken if he goes to war?
At the keyboard she lifts her graceful hand
to perform Chopin as she never could before.

And then the cannon shell that scattered him
within, across, beneath the bloodmud field,
separating limb from ragged limb,
burrowed in earth until at last it stilled.
"Never have you played so prettily,"
he almost told her, with a pensive sigh.

DEPARTURE

Always as a child I felt their gaze
from ceiling corners, broken chimneys, clay gullies.
What did they discern? That I was vulnerable,
helpless as my white blind kitten, that anyone
may know of me what I can never know?

The more I wished myself invisible
the more obtrusive my haphazard presence.
I prayed to the Sunday-school Divinity
to allow me a painless martyrdom,
to bless me with a happy accident.

Who were they, spying relentlessly?
What could they find not already known to them?
Each day they canceled one of my futures.
They warned eternity to guard its shadow.
They wore dark robes of ragged spider-thread.

Now a distant bell sounds and they turn away
and do not look back, forsaking me,
disappearing into the grove that enfolds them with silence,
into a nightfall cool and windless.

NOW THEN

The western wind grows cold and pushes
through the pines with a sound like a lone man
sweeping the distant corner of an empty warehouse.

The darkness the eventide invites pauses
to savor the details of the daily world it will devour:
hawk cry, yellow poplar leaf, diffident traffic
on the long freeway that leads from town
to the outer bedrooms and their turbulent slumbers.

The lonely half moon unveils,
silent as a snowflake falling forever,
beautiful as an abandoned child.

You sleep beside me and do not see.
You sleep beside me all aware.

IMPRIMATUR

Every moment possesses a soul indifferent
to possession, desiring nothing for itself
but simple habitation: an instant of delight,
a flash of gratitude, a single musical note
and its overtone, the echo of the intonation.
Three moments the mourning dove inspirits
with cool tones, each the soul of its moment,
none possessing it. Lonely and communal,
the music speaks but does not declare.
The tones are lonely but never alone,
like the courageous woman and her loving sisters
conversing quietly in a time of war.

ECLIPSE

The world thumbprints its shadow on the moon
and tribes and animals look out fearfully
from those low shelters they cobbled from spells
and mystic numbers to reassure themselves
the light will come again, outstretching its wings
to settle gently upon the sea and mountain.

And so the light returns, though not unchanged.
That brief intimacy with darkness altered
its nature, draining its power to display
the objects it illumined in all innocence,
and now we must examine what we cannot see.

RECESSIONAL

The staples have rusted in the warped locust posts.
Red-orange barbwire sags and trembles in the sleepiest breeze.
White-plumed thistles spear the hills
and shadowless blackbirds forage the grass.

The hand-sized terrapin, checkered yellow and black,
nudges along the cowpath to the precipice of sundown.

THE NEXT STEP

He no longer climbs the stairs to bring
firewood to the tidy white-brick hearth
and lay the oak-lengths down and draw a breath,
and give illumination to his evening.

No cat observes the kindling of a flame
with green-eyed, mesmerized intensity;
no smoke ascends into the star-flecked sky.
Tabby has died; the house is none the same.

He fumbles up the stairway empty-handed
this present hour and pauses awhile confounded
until the lungs reclaim the oxygen
he coughed away at step thirteen or so.
He counts the few stairs he has yet to go,
concludes that *this* is now and *that* was then.

PERSPECTIVE

He looks up from desk-bound labor
through the gray window to the powerline
sporting the four serious crows and beyond
to where the roofs of the town huddle
in a sociable flock and tries to imagine anew
the inner workings of the outer world.

What does the universe contain besides itself?

The imposing page with his disjointed scribble
shrinks to the size of a white rose petal,
awaiting the word he aspires to say and not to say.

RELEASE

To undergo the feeling of the vacant interstellar spaces,
ask yourself if Ramona ever thinks of you these days.
Of course she does not. Would hardly recall your name.
She may no longer live, after a fatal divorce;
maybe she became a nun or was devoured by opioids.
Maybe she decided the one thing she had never.

If only you could forget yourself yourself.

PRESENCE

Your presence fills my life the way the sun
surfaces with gold the wavelets of the lake.
As would your absence. And then the lake
would be a moondrawn sheet of polar silver.

ADAGIO, PIZZICATO

The snowbank feels the starlight on its skin
as effervescence, scintillate needlepoint
that inscribes with silence the motions of the skies.
This minute scripture keeps a strict account
of unruly meteors and the serene spin
of moon above the unresisting seas.
Starlight underscores the prescient silence
the patient snow receives and holds within.

All that is, awaits. Snow crystals gleam
at all their points, distinctly separate.
The sky has poured its diamonds upon the field
as incremental mantle, dust of light,
a presence sky-wide dispersion had concealed,
resplendent now in droplet beads of flame.

LARGO, ALLEGRO

Any hour I muse upon my love
is brief, although it may extend
throughout the bustling year with memories
of casual gesture and unconscious pose,
as when I watch how you pull on a glove
to dislocate a vine that is no friend
to your ideal garden and its ideal trees,
tendrilled ferns, and comfy shawls of moss.

Or if the thoughtful hour flashes away
more swiftly than a tender millisecond,
or at a speedy pace no clock has reckoned,
it stands remembered as a graceful day
with Susan at its center, quiet, steady,
allowing time to pass when she is ready.

LET US VISIT THE MOONLIGHT

Let us go out into the moonlight,
discarding our river-stone bungalow like a carapace.
The steps to the parterre are shelves of shadow in the moonflood slope.
The post oak guards the midnight, a sentry assigned to extra duty,
stoic but resentful, at the mercy of his thoughts.
Soon the moon will leave, collecting the night as it departs.

Dawn wind will voice the tree.

"GIVE US THIS DAY"

Jesus each day in heaven visits the cottage
where my mother tends her grateful flowers.
They sit in rocking chairs upon the porch
until the hour for her to bathe his feet.
He frowns. "Oh, let us not untidy ourselves."
"This much at least," she says, "you won't begrudge."
Now he in his turn bathes my mother's feet.

Thus, the amenities. They resume their prattle
of the rakish misadventures of Gabriel,
of the colorful sins of saints before sainthood,
missteps we all pretend to have forgotten.
They remark upon the ever-pleasant weather
and watch celestial beetles annoy the roses;
and then at sundown Jesus suggests a prayer.

CHOOSING

If you could choose your wings, would you light upon
snow-feathered vans the artist affixed to angels
in the days of angels, or the owl's shadow-silent wings,
the slate mantle of the water thrush, the epaulettes
the mockingbird sports or, forsaking the avians,
might you prefer the mica lattices of the dragonfly,
those four wings tiled with sunlight to fetch you everywhere?

With thorax upright the dragonfly thrusts as cathedral,
spiring skyward, stained-glass wings revisioning
the light, transporting it from one laurel twig
to another to another to every place where light is welcome.

Were I compact as dragonfly, those wings
would spirit me about, scattering the day
into sudden showers of droplet diamonds.

AFTERWARD PRESENCE

Like a quality of light as yet unmanifest,
everywhere knowable but everywhere unseen:
so, your presence when you go from a room
wherein you were reading a favorite story
or along the patch of hellebores when you leave them
to drink at leisure the water you bestow:

That is to say, a presence that absence cannot erase,
a manner of being where being is removed;
that is, the palpable echo of words unspoken:
I know that you are there, wherever you have been.

In a further hour your nonpresence will diminish;
the colors of the blooms will darken imperceptibly,
displaying another aspect of your present absence.
The night will embrace your absence to complete its presence.

THE DREAM AND I

The dream and I were not on speaking terms,
but when it died I walked alone and homeless.
All those whom it deserted with its demise
roamed the world as inconsolable orphans,
searching each another's features for signs,
and finally abandoning all hope.
The poor suffered less than did the wealthy,
learning young that dreams do not come true,
learning afterward that nightmares do.

THE HISTORY OF STUDY

I study closely the volumes and monuments
but learn no secrets. Like the mother who shields
her child from the drunken spouse, every instance
of its being the past protects, and yields
to close examination only dim hints,
muffled semishapes that clover fields
blanket, wide and silent and intense.

Perhaps it would be fitting to genuflect
in reverence to History, landscape
featureless, horizonless, and mute,
a state of being that borders upon the state
of nonbeing; and then declare devotion:
"Thank you, brutal Parent, for my world."

FINAL CONCERT

Within a sweltering twilight, the omen of autumn:

as when an orchestra sounds a pianissimo chord

in low register, absorbed more than heard, or heard

only in expectancy, our senses poised, awaiting

the downstroke, our breathing not yet unison,

the tremulous quiver of wing as moth settles to leaf,

the sigh of laurel leaf as it receives the moth:

And now the music begins, adagio, sultry, immersive as sunset,

the Concerto surrendering to nighttime its sweet season.

ABOUT THE AUTHOR

Fred Chappell was the author of more than thirty volumes of poetry and prose, including *Midquest,* a quartet of long poems that he described as "something like a verse novel," and *I Am One of You Forever,* the first in a tetralogy of novels known as the Kirkman Family Cycle. Honors bestowed upon his work include the Bollingen Prize in Poetry from Yale University, the Aiken Taylor Award for Modern American Poetry, the T. S. Eliot Award for Creative Writing, the Thomas Wolfe Prize, the World Fantasy Award for Short Fiction, and the Award in Literature from the National Institute of Arts and Letters. Seven of his poetry books received the Roanoke-Chowan Award from the North Carolina Literary and Historical Association. His fiction has been translated into more than a dozen languages and his novel *Dagon* received the Best Foreign Book Award from the Académie Française. A native of Canton in the mountains of western North Carolina, Chappell was the state's poet laureate from 1997 to 2002 and an English professor at the University of North Carolina at Greensboro for forty years. He passed away in January 2024 at the age of eighty-seven.

Printed in the USA
CPSIA information can be obtained
at www.ICGtesting.com
CBHW020043121124
17273CB00002B/110